Cults & Other Beliefs

9780570097532

by Bruce Frederickson

Teachers Guide

Contents

Session 1	What Do I Believe	3
Session 2	Established Cults	8
Session 3	Modern Christian, Eastern and Science Cults	12
Session 4	Satanic Cults	17

Prepared by the staff of the Board for Parish Services, The Lutheran Church—Missouri Synod

Written by Bruce Frederickson
Edited by Thomas J. Doyle
Editorial assistant: Phoebe Wellman

Write to Library for the Blind, 1333 S. Kirkwood Road, St. Louis, MO 63122-7295 to obtain *Cults and Other Beliefs* (Teachers Guide) in braille or in large print for the visually impaired.

Scripture quotations in this publication are from The Holy Bible: NEW INTERNATIONAL VERSION, copyright © 1973, 1979, 1984 by the International Bible Society. Used by permission of Zondervan Bible Publishers.

Copyright © 1990 Concordia Publishing House
3558 S. Jefferson Avenue, St. Louis, MO 63118-3968
Manufactured in the United States of America

All rights reserved. No part of this publication may be reproduced, stored in a retrieval system, or transmitted, in any form or by any means, electronic, mechanical, photocopying, recording, or otherwise, without the prior written permission of Concordia Publishing House.

1 2 3 4 5 6 7 8 9 10   MID   99 98 97 96 95 94 93 92 91 90

What Do I Believe?

DISCOVERY POINT

God reveals Himself to us in His Word. By the power of the Holy Spirit working through the Word, God creates and sustains saving faith in Jesus Christ, thereby providing forgiveness of sins and eternal life.

OBJECTIVES

That by the power of the Holy Spirit working through God's Word the students will

1. describe the doctrines of the Christian church which distinguish it from other religions and cults;
2. compare saving faith in Jesus with religious rituals;
3. describe the danger of groups which emphasize rituals over faith in Christ Jesus;
4. give thanks to God for the salvation He provides through faith in Christ alone;
5. confess their faith in Jesus as their Savior from sin, death, and the power of the devil.

MATERIALS

- [ ] Bibles
- [ ] Student Book
- [ ] *Lutheran Worship* or *The Lutheran Hymnal*
- [ ] pencils or pens

Optional
- [ ] poster board
- [ ] markers
- [ ] tempera paint
- [ ] newsprint

OVERVIEW OF THIS COURSE

It is important to prepare students for the attacks that may be made upon their faith lives by exposing them to the false beliefs of cults and other religions. It is imperative that students (1) understand what they believe and why they believe it, and (2) understand what others believe.

You may wish to order the following resources to assist you in preparing to teach this course: *Which Way Is the Right Way: A Study of Christianity, Cults, and Other Religions* and the Response series (12 booklets), both available from Concordia Publishing House.

"Religion" and "faith" are the topics of session 1. In session 2, established cults, Jehovah Witness, Mormon, and Christian Science, are examined. Newer cults and their teachings, including the Moonies, Hare Krishna, and Scientology, are discussed in session 3. In the fourth and final session, Satanism, a dangerous threat to the faith and life of every Christian, is examined.

The Teachers Guide will assist you as you prepare to describe cults and other religions, and compare them to Christianity by examining where they depart from the truth of God's Word. Remind your students often that in Christ, God entered into the world and offered redemption to all people from sin, death, and eternal separation from Him. God accomplished this miracle for all people as His Son suffered and died on the cross. The cross should be the focal point for each lesson. Urge students to keep their eyes on Jesus **(Heb. 12:2).** All other religions are self-constructed, and therefore contain no legitimate redeemer.

SESSION 1: GETTING STARTED

Confirmation students can spend much time studying "religion" without understanding "faith." "Faith" is a gift of God, not simply intellectual knowledge. Allow ample time to talk about the difference between "faith" and "religion." Some people view Christianity as no more than a "religion." Actually, religion is only a series of rituals and actions. People could go through the same rituals, but have completely different invisible beliefs or motivations in their hearts. Others recognize Christianity as "faith" in a merciful and loving God who sent His only Son, Jesus, to live, suffer, and die on a cross, and rise victorious from death proclaiming His victory over sin, death, and the power of the devil.

It is possible to be religious without being Christian. Some people feel that it is possible to have a personal faith in Jesus Christ as Savior, without necessarily going through the motions of religious rituals. Emphasize the importance of worshiping regularly with other members of the body of Christ.

Faith and religion are both important to Christians. "Saving faith" in Jesus Christ is a gift which the Holy Spirit creates in the hearts of individuals. While the religious activities of individuals may vary, there are certain responses which flow from faith, Bible reading, worship, and prayer.

OPENING WORSHIP

Pray the following prayer for steadfast faith found on page 125 of *Lutheran Worship*.

Almighty God, our heavenly Father, of your tender love towards us sinners You have given us Your Son that, believing in Him, we might have everlasting life. Continue to grant us Your Holy Spirit that we may remain steadfast in this faith to the end and come to life everlasting; through Jesus Christ, our Lord. Amen.

Since this lesson will discuss faith, it would be appropriate for you to lead students in confessing their faith in the words of the Apostles' Creed.

INTRODUCING THE LESSON

1. Teach students the Swimming to Europe witnessing activity. Duplicate the line drawings in the appendix and the following outline, if necessary.

a. There is an ocean of sin that separated us from God.

b. Suppose a person wanted to cross the Atlantic Ocean from North America to Europe. To cross the ocean, a person who could not swim (A), might wade until the water became too deep. Then he/she would drown. A mediocre swimmer (B), might swim three miles if he/she were desperate enough. Then he/she too would drown. An Olympic swimmer might be able to swim 30 miles. But eventually, even this super athlete would drown. All three swimmers would die. There's no difference.

c. An ocean of sin separates us from God. Even worse, the island on which we are standing, our life on this earth, is sinking. Yet, to get to God on our own would be just as impossible for us as swimming across the Atlantic. It may seem to us that a very wicked criminal (A), would not have much chance to earn God's love. Person (B), who sometimes goes to church and tries to be a good person, might seem to go a little farther. But even person (C), a very, very good person according to human standards, cannot be good enough to reach God on his/her own. In **Matt. 5:48** God says, **"Be perfect!"** None of us are perfect or can be perfect. In God's eyes, there is no difference. Every person on earth deserves to die eternally. No one is good. We all sin.

d. To cross the Atlantic Ocean, we need a ship or an airplane. The only way for sinners to get to God is by faith in Jesus. He is our "Life Raft." We "get in the boat" by trusting Him for forgiveness of sins and eternal life.

2. Write "Christianity" on the chalkboard. Ask students to write a brief definition of "Christianity" on a sheet of notebook paper. Discuss the definitions. Ask, **What differentiates Christianity from other religions?** Help students to understand that in all religions other than Christianity people must place their trust or faith in themselves and their own abilities. Christians place their complete trust in what Jesus did for them on the cross.

3. Discuss the importance of the Apostles' Creed. Ask, **Why is it important for Christians to know the Apostles' Creed and confess its words?** When Christians confess the Apostles' Creed, they are united with Christians throughout the ages who have confessed and continue to confess Jesus Christ as their Lord and Savior. Ask, **When do we recite the Apostles' Creed during worship?** Some students may say that either the Apostles' or Nicene Creed are confessed during every worship service. Remind students that the Apostles' Creed was probably confessed at their baptism. **Why is it important for the Creed to be spoken at a baptism?** The Apostles' Creed is a confession of the faith into which the person is baptized.

4. Take a quick trip into the church's sanctuary. Discuss the different symbols of faith in the church (baptismal font, stained-glass windows, altar, etc.).

TEACHING ACTIVITIES

True or FALSE

Read and discuss each of the statements made by the characters at the top of the page. Tell students that each of the statements is false. Ask students to make the false statements true either individually on a sheet of notebook paper or as a class on the chalkboard. You may wish to return to this activity after you have completed instructions to evaluate students' understanding of the concepts, faith, and religion. Some suggestions for making the statements true are as follows: (1) It is possible to be religious without being Christian. For example, Buddhists, Hindus, and Moslems are religious people. (2) Faith is a gift which the Holy Spirit creates in the hearts of individuals. (3) Religion is a series of rituals and actions performed by people. (4) There are poor reasons for joining a church (i.e. to advance oneself professionally, to earn God's love and respect, etc.). (5) Although the Holy Spirit creates faith and sustains faith in people who hear God's Word, people who attend worship don't necessarily have saving faith. (6) The Holy Spirit works to sustain faith through the means of grace which include hearing and reading God's Word and attending the Lord's Supper. (7) There is a great difference between Christianity and other religions. All other religions rely on "what I can do," while Christians rely on "what God has done for us through Christ Jesus." (8) Faith and religion have different meanings. Refer to "Getting Started." (9) Although sincere faith in beliefs, others, and oneself may be commendable, the only absolutely essential faith is faith that relies totally on Jesus Christ for forgiveness of sins and eternal life. (10) It is extremely important to know what you believe before studying what others believe, so you can appreciate and defend your beliefs and determine where others deviate from your beliefs.

WHAT IS FAITH?

1. Answers will vary as students describe "faith." After students have had the opportunity to describe faith, you may wish to share the following quote from a sermon by Martin Luther.

Faith is the yes of the heart, a conviction on which one stakes one's life. On what does faith rest? On Christ . . . this faith does not grow by our own powers. On the contrary, the Holy Spirit is present and writes it on the heart.

2. Faith and religion are both important to Christians. "Saving faith" in Jesus Christ is a gift which the Holy Spirit creates in the hearts of individuals. Through faith in Jesus, God offers forgiveness of sins and eternal life to all people. Religion is the service and worship of God or a god, including attitudes, beliefs, and practices.

3. *Now faith is being sure of what we hope for and certain of what we do not see* **(Heb. 11:1).** The writer of Hebrews describes faith by providing a brief biographical sketch of some of God's Old Testament people. For example, Abraham continued to have faith in God's promise of "a great nation" despite the fact that his wife was unable to have children.

Student answers will vary. Some students may have demonstrated a faith similar to that of the Old Testament people as they have been confronted by various problems and concerns in their lives. Allow students to share experiences freely.

4. After reading **Matt. 8:5–13,** ask, **How would you describe the Roman centurion's faith in Jesus?** Obviously, the officer had heard about Jesus and the things He had done from others. Since the centurion was in charge of Roman soldiers, he understood authority, and the supreme authority of Jesus over all things, including disease. He had faith in the fact that Jesus could heal his servant.

THE OBJECT OF FAITH

1. Ask for a student to volunteer to read the letter from Desert Pete. Answers to the questions will vary.

2. This story describes faith in Desert Pete, an unknown character. You can never see, touch, taste, or smell faith. God's Word not only defines faith, it also describes it. Faith doesn't exist in and by itself, instead it only exists in someone or something.

You must have water before you can prime a pump. Similarly, you must have faith before it can be nurtured and grow. Like the water left by Desert Pete, faith is a gift. After reading **Rom. 10:14–17,** explain to students that saving faith, created by the working of the Holy Spirit through the Word, only exists in the person and work of Jesus Christ.

Faith is primed by the Holy Spirit through the means of grace, God's Word and the Sacraments. Although saving faith can only be created by the Holy Spirit and received by people through faith, it can be rejected by people. Some people receive the gift of saving faith, and their faith remains rooted in Jesus Christ as long as things are going well in their lives. They are in control of situations in their lives, and nothing is introduced to challenge their faith. But when troubles and challenges confront these people, they reject faith in Jesus Christ and allow other people and things to become the object of their faith.

If time permits read **Matt. 13:1–23,** the parable of the sower. In this parable Jesus compares faith which is not firmly rooted in the Good News of Jesus Christ, to faith which is firmly rooted in the Gospel.

3. If faith was mere intellectual knowledge, then we could say that the devil also has faith. The "fear" which Luther describes in the explanation to the Commandments means to have reverential awe of God. The fear of God produced by faith in Christ Jesus is very different from the fear (fright) exhibited by the devil **(James 2:19).**

4. The object of our faith is the Triune God. In the Apostles' Creed we confess faith in God's creating ability, in the redemption Christ earned for us on the cross, and in the Holy Spirit who creates and sustains faith in our hearts.

Through faith Christians have certainty of eternal life. In the Bible, God assures believers that Christ earned eternal life for them. Ask, **Many other religions also believe in an "after life." How is belief in eternal life different for a Christian?** Eternal life is certain for a Christian, because it is a gift from God earned by Christ's death on the cross, not by our own goodness or the good things we have tried to do **(Rom. 6:23, Eph. 2:8–9).** All other religions teach that there is something people must do to earn or merit eternal life. Only Christianity teaches of a never-ending life which begins with faith and continues beyond the grave!

Illustrate a Christian's certainty of eternal life and the uncertainty of other religions with the following story:

There are only two religions in the world.

You're walking along a road one day and fall into a very deep hole. You start scratching, jumping, and shouting as you try to get out. You hear a noise in a corner of the hole. You discover a snake curled up in the corner, a deadly poisonous snake. Now you really begin to panic.

Along comes a Muslim. He looks down into the hole and says, "Ah, dear brother, I see you've fallen into a hole, and I am indeed sorry for you. But all in this world is Allah's will. This too must be part of his will for you. Submit. Resign yourself to his will." He goes on his way and leaves you in the hole.

Along comes a Hindu. He notices you in the hole, looks down and says, "Ah, dear brother, I see you've fallen into a hole. I am indeed sorry for you. But Nirvanah is the goal of all people, to be absorbed into the godhead. And we reach that by contemplation. Contemplate." And he goes on his way and leaves you in the hole.

Along comes a Buddhist, and upon seeing that you are in the hole, says, "Oh, dear brother, I see that you have fallen into a hole, and I am indeed sorry for you. The eightfold path to goodness is the way to God. When you have perfected all eight you will reach it. Obviously you haven't reached that point yet. Contemplate and perfect them." And he goes on his way, leaving you in the hole.

A follower of Confucius comes along and says, "Ah, dear brother. I see you've fallen into a hole. I am indeed sorry for you, but all in this world is Yin and Yang, the cosmic principles in this dualistic philosophy, and it all comes out in the end." And he walks away shaking his head.

Finally, along comes Jesus Christ. He sees you in the hole, and without a word, jumps in with you. The noise of Him boosting you out of the hole excites the snake, and the snake strikes, and bites Jesus. Jesus falls dead, but you walk away free.

The two religions of the world are the religion of God and the religion of people. All religions other than Christianity leave you in the hole. Although they may offer you some form of solace through meditation, contemplation, or working to perfect yourself, only Jesus Christ got into the hole of sin for you. He ended up dead, in order to get you out alive. But by His resurrection He closed the hole forever!

5. Invite individual students to share their response to a lonely friend. While many people say they have "faith" in God, their faith is limited to some time far in the future. Christ offers us faith for now and forever.

PUT YOUR MONEY WHERE YOUR MOUTH IS

Discuss the meaning of the phrase, "Put your money where your mouth is." Read **Matt. 15:1–9.** After reading these verses ask the students, **How did Jesus react to people whose faith was only words?** Jesus condemns those people for substituting the true faith with faith in themselves and their own rules. Read **James 2:14–26.** Ask, **What is the proof of a person's faith?** Good works follow faith. Faith without deeds is dead.

Ask a volunteer to read the story about Blondin, the tightrope walker. After reading the story discuss the questions. Answers will vary. Remind students that some people think that faith is simply to know about Jesus, while others may think that it is enough to say that they trust in Jesus. But as demonstrated in the story of Blondin, the evidence of faith is in the trusting. We demonstrate our faith by "sitting in the chair."

Read Luther's comments about faith from his sermon on **Gal. 4:1–5.** Ask, **Why does Luther describe faith as "the yes of the heart."** Emphasize the Holy Spirit as the active agent in creating and sustaining faith, and people as the passive agents who can only receive the faith which God offers by His grace. The Holy Spirit continues to be our faith power source. For faith-strengthening power, all people are invited to read, study, and hear God's Word, through which the Holy Spirit works.

DO YOU KNOW WHAT YOU BELIEVE?

1. Read the story of the American Bankers Association. Then, ask your students to offer possible reasons for showing the counterfeit money to the students only on the last day of class. In order for the tellers to identify counterfeit money, they must first know the identifying marks of real money.

Ask, **Why is it important to know your own beliefs thoroughly before you begin to study other beliefs?** We may become confused if we don't understand our own belief and its source.

2. Urge volunteers to read their brief witness of faith to the accident victim. Stress the value of being able to articulate their faith in Christ Jesus. Since most students will know **John 3:16,** suggest using it as an outline for a personal witness. Read **1 John 5:13** and tell students that the main reason the Bible was written was to provide us with certainty of eternal life through Jesus Christ. Even though Christians confess faith in Jesus, many don't possess the comfort of the certainty God provides in His Word. They might not realize that Jesus paid their full entrance fee into heaven. He died for all **(2 Cor. 5:14–15)** and by His death and resurrection paid our debt in full. Tell students, **The world is full of victims suffering from the guilt of their sin. God provides opportunities for you to comfort them as you share His Good News of forgiveness and eternal life through Jesus Christ. Only through the Gospel can people find true, everlasting comfort.**

TO REVIEW AND REMEMBER

Lead students in a review of the three articles of the Apostles' Creed and their explanations. You may wish to assign one or more of the articles to be memorized as a homework assignment.

FAMILY TIME

Assign students either one or both of the Family Time activities to be completed with their families during the next week.

ENRICHMENT ACTIVITIES

1. Have each student design a poster illustrating saving faith in Christ Jesus. Hang the posters in the classroom or in the hallways of the church.

2. Divide your class into groups of five or six students. Distribute markers or paints and a large sheet of newsprint. Ask students to design and draw a mural depicting **Hebrews 11.**

3. Return to the false statements introduced at the beginning of this lesson. As a quiz evaluating students' understanding of the concepts taught during this lesson, ask students to make each statement true. Write the true statements on a sheet of notebook paper.

4. Invite a convert from another religion or cult to describe how his/her life has changed since receiving the gift of faith in Christ Jesus. Ask the convert how he/she came to faith.

CLOSING WORSHIP

Sing or read the words of "My Faith Looks Trustingly" (*LW* 378, *TLH* 394).

Lead students or ask them to volunteer to close with a prayer thanking God for His gift of faith in Christ Jesus.

Established Cults

DISCOVERY POINT

God clearly reveals Himself in His Word offering His promise of forgiveness of sins and eternal life through faith in Christ Jesus.

OBJECTIVES

That by the power of the Holy Spirit working through God's Word the students will

1. confess the uniqueness and the eternal truthfulness of Jesus Christ as revealed by God in His Word;
2. describe the origin and teaching of the following cults: Jehovah's Witness, Mormon, and Christian Science;
3. witness their faith in Christ Jesus to non-Christians;
4. give thanks to God for the certainty of eternal life He provides through faith in Christ Jesus.

MATERIALS

- [ ] Bibles
- [ ] Student Books
- [ ] *Lutheran Worship* or *The Lutheran Hymnal*
- [ ] pencils and/or pens

Optional
- [ ] various resource books including atlas, encyclopedia, dictionary, magazines, and a Bible
- [ ] poster paper
- [ ] markers
- [ ] two batches of cookies
- [ ] medicines designed to relieve itching (e.g. calamine lotion, athlete foot spray, etc.)
- [ ] 3 × 5 index cards
- [ ] *An Open Letter to a Jehovah's Witness*, available from Concordia Tract Mission (Concordia Publishing House)
- [ ] *Book of Mormon*

SESSION 2: GETTING STARTED

The popularity of "cults" poses a serious problem and threat to Christianity. While cults and their practices may appear to be legitimate religions, they often use deceit and "psychologically coercive" methods in recruiting individuals and fostering dependence on members.

Understand the distinction between "cults" which have splintered from other groups, and "occult" which means "secret" or "hidden." "Occult" refers to the practice of fortunetelling or magic, which often involves the influence of evil spiritual powers. Although many "cults" may use the "occult" these terms are not synonymous.

The false and dangerous teachings of most cults only prove the truth of **Eccl. 1:9, ". . . there is nothing new under the sun."** Cults attack Christianity's most important teaching, the person and work of Jesus Christ. In fact, immediately following the Lord's ascension into heaven, cults began to develop as people attempted to answer the question, "Who is Jesus Christ?" These attacks are not new. Instead of depending upon God's Word as the source and norm of all teaching about the person and work of Jesus Christ, people began to speculate based upon their own rational and intellectual capabilities. The false and destructive teachings of cults have been promoted for centuries. New cults merely perpetuate ancient heresies.

OPENING WORSHIP

Ask students, **What can you do if you develop a terrible itchy rash? What can you do to find relief from the itching?** Show students the bottles of medication. Say, **Each of these bottles contain medicine to provide relief from itching. If you have a terrible itchy rash, it feels wonderful to put the medicine on the rash. Relief is almost instantaneous.**

How is sin like an itchy rash? There is no relief from sin without help. Ask, **What relief does God**

provide from sin? God provided His Son, Jesus, as our relief from sin. All that we need to know about the person and work of Jesus in order to receive the forgiveness of sins and eternal life God reveals to us in His Word, the Bible.

Read **2 Tim. 3:12–17.** St. Paul shares with his brother, Timothy, the remedy for the painful itching caused by sin.

Sing or speak the words of "Thy Strong Word" (*LW* 328) or "How Precious Is the Book Divine" (*LW* 332, *TLH* 285).

INTRODUCING THE LESSON

1. Place a variety of resource materials on a table (i.e. magazines, various textbooks, encyclopedia, dictionary, atlas, thesaurus, Bible, etc.). Discuss the importance of each of the resources, saving the Bible for last. Ask students, **How are these resource materials alike?** After students have had an opportunity to respond, ask, **How are they different?**

Look in the cover pages to find the names of authorities who wrote the various resource materials. Then, direct students' attention to the Bible. Say, **The writing of the Bible was inspired and directed by the ultimate authority!** Tell students that the ultimate authority, God Himself, provides all that we need in order to receive the blessings of forgiveness and sins and eternal life in His Word, the Bible.

2. Bake two batches of cookies. Burn one batch and bake the other batch according to the recipe. Tell students that you brought them a treat to share before class. Pass out the burnt cookies. As students share that the cookies are burnt, say, **Sorry, I decided that I didn't need to follow the recipe in baking the cookies. I guess the oven was too hot or I left them in the oven too long. I should have followed the recipe instead of guessing.** After discussing the importance of following a recipe rather than guessing, tell students that cults have often been established because people didn't look to God's Word as the authority by which they could find out all they needed to know about the person and work of Jesus. Instead, people depend on their own intellectual knowledge, which is tainted by sin, to try to find out about the person and work of Jesus.

Share the good batch of cookies after the discussion.

3. Ask students to report on Family Time activity 1 from session 1 if it was assigned.

4. Put students in one of three groups as they arrive. Place on a table resource materials which contains information about the following cults: Mormon, Christian Scientist, Jehovah's Witness. Tell students to find interesting facts about their assigned cult and write them on index cards. Ask them to share the information they find during the session.

ITCHING EARS

Ask students to read the speech bubbles in each of the frames at the beginning of Session 2 in the Student Book. Lead a discussion using the questions concerning itching. Allow students to offer possible suggestions as to how the first two frames are related to the third frame. Accept any answers students may generate.

Ask a student to read **2 Tim. 4:3–4** to the class. Ask, **How are the itching ears described in 2 Timothy similar to the itching caused by a rash or a disease?** Remind students that there are two ways for relief of itching: (1) scratching, or (2) medicine. People often want their ears scratched by things they want to hear. This leads people to listen to the heretical doctrine of false teachers. **"They will turn their ears away from the truth and turn aside to myths,"** if the myths explain or describe something they wish to hear. Itching ears cause people to create gods and religion that meet their whims.

The "itching ear" matching exercise is designed to introduce students to words that will be used throughout this session and subsequent sessions. Do not give the students the answers. Instead allow students to use resource materials (dictionary and encyclopedia) to match each itching ear word to its description or definition. If resource materials are not available, define the words as you teach the information in the session and ask students to return to the words at the end of the session. The answers are as follows: 1. cult, c. "splinter group" from the Christian church; 2. heresy, a. an opinion or teaching contrary to the church's teaching; 3. Mormon, b. followers of the teaching of Joseph Smith; 4. Pelagians, f. believed Jesus was true God, but not true man; 5. Arians, e. followers of an ancient heresy condemned at the council in Nicea in A.D. 325; 6. Jehovah's Witness, g. religion whose members meet in "Kingdom Halls" and distribute literature door-to-door across the United States and the world; 7. Christian Scientist, d. believes in teachings contained in Mary Baker Eddy's book, *Science and Health with Key to the Scriptures.*

CULTS BEGIN

Allow students to answer the questions in the introductory paragraph. A cult is a "splinter group" from the Christian church or another religion. Cults form in various ways. For example, they may form when an individual or group of individuals become angry with their own church, are misled by a charismatic personality, do not know what they believe, are not able to defend the fundamental teachings of their church, etc. Students may know individuals who are members of cults. Tell students they will learn details about each of these cults so that they can minister effectively to individuals who may be members of one of them.

1. Write "Arianism" on the chalkboard. Tell students that Arianism is an ancient heresy started by a man named Arius. Ask students to volunteer reading portions of this section. The longest section of the Nicene Creed is the Second Article. Within this article the orthodox Christian church made a firm confession about the Scriptural understanding of the person and work of Jesus Christ. Sometimes it takes great detail to avoid misunderstanding.

2. After reading about the Pelagians, ask students to compare the Arian heresy to the Pelagian heresy. You may wish to make a chart on the chalkboard or on poster board listing characteristics of both the ancient cultic heresies and the modern cultic heresies. This chart can be used for the purpose of comparison throughout this session and the two subsequent sessions.

3. The Athanasian Creed emphasizes the doctrine of the Trinity.

4. You may wish to show the students the Book of Concord, which contains the confessions of The Lutheran Church—Missouri Synod.

Our enemy, the devil, has caused people to doubt since the fall of people into sin.

JEHOVAH'S WITNESSES

If you are making a chart of the various heresies, write Jehovah's Witnesses in the next column.

1. Ask students to read silently these two paragraphs.

Point out that Russell's religion had elements of Arianism and anti-trinitarianism.

2. **How could a cult which teaches false doctrines continue to grow? What appeal would the Jehovah's Witnesses have for Christian people?**

3. Kingdom Halls of the Jehovah's Witnesses are designed more like lecture halls than worship centers. Jehovah's Witnesses pray, sing songs, read Scripture, and listen to sermons or lectures. Most of their activities appear more like classroom activities than worship services. Whenever Jehovah's Witnesses visit their Kingdom Hall for a meeting they first report about the time they spent in witnessing and the quantity of literature distributed. Leaders are appointed from the rank and file of the group annually and are called "overseers."

4. Jehovah's Witnesses spend a great deal of time studying the Bible and place a great deal of emphasis on memorizing Scripture. Therefore, they seem to know their Bible quite well. But quoting isolated passages from the Bible out of context is not really Bible study. We must understand God's Word by its context.

Demonstrate to your students how Jehovah's Witnesses quote the Bible so that it says anything they want it to say. Ask your students to cover up the first and last parts of **Ps. 14:1,** and read the remaining words. Now ask, **Does the Bible say, "there is no God?"** Of course it does, but this is not God's intent in this verse. It is clear from the context which was omitted, that the "fool" says there is no God. Point out to students that this is what happens when Scripture is quoted at random, without regard to God's intent.

5. Ask, **How would you respond to a Jehovah's Witness who said that Jesus isn't God or that Jesus didn't rise from the dead?** Refer to Luther's Small Catechism, and remind students that the Bible gives Jesus divine names **(John 20:28),** divine attributes or qualities **(John 1:1, Heb. 13:8),** divine works **(John 1:3, Matt. 9:6),** and divine honor and glory **(John 5:23).**

If a Jehovah's Witness approaches you with the argument that Jesus is not equal to the Father, be sure to point out **John 5:22–23, 17:22.** Since the Father and the Son are both part of the Godhead, those who fail to honor the Son, also fail to honor the Father.

6–7. When Jehovah's Witnesses knock at your door, they seldom state their false teachings directly. Instead they cloak dangerous false teachings within arguments about deplorable world conditions or some social problem. Gradually they attempt to draw you into their unique brand of "Bible-Bingo," addressing only certain passages which they use to support their beliefs.

For those who are interested, several short tracts are available from Concordia Tract Mission to help people deal with Jehovah's Witnesses. One tract, *An Open Letter to a Jehovah's Witness*, can actually be given to a Jehovah's Witness who calls at your door.

MORMONS

1–2. Since the Mormons regularly advertise in magazines and on television, your students may be more aware of this group than the Jehovah's Witnesses. They may even know Mormons personally and agree that "they are nice people." But how "nice" someone is, is not as important as what they believe about Christ, forgiveness of sins, and eternal life in heaven. Ask, **Why are the church's teachings about Christ, forgiveness of sins, and eternal life so important to Christians?**

3. Mormons claim that their *Book of Mormon* is "more" authoritative than the Holy Bible. You may wish to obtain a copy of the *Book of Mormon* from the library and read several passages allowing students to evaluate what it says. Mormonism resembles the Arian and anti-Trinitarian heresies.

4. Like Jehovah's Witnesses, Mormons deny the deity of Christ and the doctrine of the Trinity. Special

ceremonies conducted in their temples are said to convey special blessings reserved for special people. Among these ceremonies are "baptism of the dead," and the "sealing of marriages for time and eternity."

Mormons await a reunion with their earthly family, much more than they anticipate a reunion with Christ. Mormons teach "works-righteousness" which offers no comfort or certainty. For the Mormon, forgiveness of sins and eternal life are based not on the merits of Christ, but rather on the efforts of the individual **(Eph. 2:8–9)**. The blood Christ shed on the cross offers no comfort for Mormons.

CHRISTIAN SCIENCE

1. While not as well known as the first two cults, some of your students may have seen a Christian Science reading room or heard of their famous newspaper and radio program, *The Christian Science Monitor*. It is difficult to determine exactly what a Christian Scientist actually believes.

2. Like Mormons, Christian Scientists elevate another book above the Bible. Their source of authority is not God's Word but the writings of Mary Baker Eddy.

Like the Mormons and Jehovah's Witnesses, Christian Scientists deny the deity of Christ. According to Christian Scientists, Christ's sacrificial death on the cross for the sins of the world has no value. All cults attack Christianity at its center—namely Jesus Christ and His substitutionary payment for sin (the person and work of Jesus).

According to the Bible, the sinfulness of people originated with the fall **(Rom. 5:12)** and caused all sickness. Christian Scientists deny the existence of sin and evil. They suggest that evil is only an illusion. For Christian Scientists, healing is the result of "manipulating" certain principles correctly. When healing fails, these principles have not been used properly.

Study with students Jesus' announcement of forgiveness of sins and healing of the paralytic **(Matt. 9:1–8)**. Only Jesus can forgive sin. Only Jesus can heal. Only Jesus is to be worshiped and served. All accounts of Jesus' healings emphasize Jesus as the healer, not "correct methodology" or "metaphysical manipulation" of certain principles.

TO REVIEW AND REMEMBER

Continue reviewing the three articles of the Apostles' Creed. You may wish to assign the articles and their explanation as a memory assignment.

FAMILY TIME

These Scripture passages are chosen to help the student and his/her family discover the Biblical teachings about the person and work of Jesus. Ask students to make notes with their parents on any verses which might be helpful when witnessing to cult members.

ENRICHMENT ACTIVITIES

1. Discuss the following questions. Ask students to answer the questions on notebook paper first, if you choose.

a. **Why could the study of cults be dangerous?** We can be confused, curious, and mistakenly lured into a cult. Because cults often use deceptive recruiting techniques, urge students to be on guard against them. Remind students of the warning in **1 John 4:1**.

b. **What is attractive about a strong leader who tells you exactly what to do?** Strong leadership attracts insecure or dependent people removing from them the burden of responsibility.

c. **What is the most dangerous isolation required by a cult?** The most dangerous isolation is from God's Word.

2. Caution your students against ridiculing cult members. In doing so, they may "turn off" the cult member and close the door for future witnessing opportunities. Roleplay situations where a cult member shares a false, unbiblical teaching. Allow a student to respond with a witness of his/her faith to the student playing the cult member.

3. Design warning signs against specific heretical teachings of the cults studied in this session. Signs may resemble the familiar "no smoking" signs.

4. Design posters which show the fundamental teachings of the Christian church (Trinity, resurrection of Jesus from the dead, baptism, Holy Communion, Holy Scripture, etc.)

CLOSING WORSHIP

Confess together the words of the Nicene Creed. Pray the Lord's Prayer together.

Modern Christian, Eastern and Science Cults

DISCOVERY POINT

God promises forgiveness of sins and abundant life, now and in eternity through faith in Jesus.

OBJECTIVES

That by the power of the Spirit the students will

1. confess Jesus Christ as the only means for receiving forgiveness of sins and abundant, eternal life;
2. describe the identifying characteristics of cults and use them as a rule by which to measure religious groups;
3. resist the lures and attacks of cults through faith strengthened by God's Word;
4. witness their faith in Jesus to unbelievers;
5. praise God for His gift of faith in Christ Jesus and the means by which He sustains that faith.

MATERIALS

- [ ] Bibles
- [ ] Student Book
- [ ] *Lutheran Worship* or *The Lutheran Hymnal*
- [ ] pen or pencil

Optional
- [ ] construction paper
- [ ] magazines and/or newspapers
- [ ] glue
- [ ] scissors
- [ ] notebook paper
- [ ] *How to Respond to the New Christian Religions*, available from CPH
- [ ] *How to Respond to the Science Religions*, available from CPH
- [ ] *How to Respond to the Eastern Religions*, available from CPH

OPENING WORSHIP

Read **Rom. 12:1–2.** Then sing "Take My Life, O Lord, Renew" (*LW* 404, *TLH* 400). Ask students to concentrate on the things they can do with their hands, feet, lips, and lives to serve Jesus, demonstrating their sincere desire to allow Christ to guide all they think, do, and say.

INTRODUCING THE LESSON

1. Ask, **What prominent teaching of the Christian church do most cults attack first?** Cults usually attack the person and work of Jesus Christ. Ask students to give examples of how cults attack the church's doctrine of Jesus.

Then say, **In preparing to play against another athletic team it is helpful to watch your opponent play someone else. High school, college, and professional sport teams regularly send scouts and/or review video recordings of their opponents to learn their strategy. Similarly, we must understand the strategy of cults. Cults usually attack our faith in Jesus Christ by answering the question, "Who is Jesus Christ?" using sources other than the Bible.** Explain that the word "orthodox" means "straight teaching" and refers to the teaching derived from the Bible by the Christian church.

2. Read **Acts 6–7** or briefly tell the story of Stephen including the following events. Stephen was appointed to serve tables and arrested because of the great signs he did among the people. He delivered a bold speech before the official Jewish court. As the "punch line" of his sermon he accused his listeners of having betrayed and murdered their Savior **(7:51–53)** As a violent reaction to the sermon, Stephen was dragged out of the city and stoned to death.

Ask, **Why did they stone Stephen? What words of Stephen's sermon caused them to rush at him? Why?** The Jews at that time believed that Jesus' followers were members of a cult. The Jewish leaders wanted to get rid of them. **In what ways do we react similarly toward cults today? In what ways do we react differently?**

3. Suggest that several students roleplay two cult members visiting the home of one of the other stu-

dents. Allow the class to make suggestions of things the cult members might say and how a Christian might respond. Have the students find Scripture verses to answer the possible questions of a cult member. Remind students that most cults attack the person and work of Jesus. Allow the students to roleplay the situation. Allow time after the roleplay to provide the players with feedback.

REVIEWING THE ORIGIN OF CULTS

Have students work independently or in small groups to complete the crossword puzzle. The puzzle will provide students with a review of the information taught in the first two sessions. Allow students time to complete the puzzle. After students complete the puzzle give them the answers. Provide additional background information as needed. The answers to the crossword puzzle are as follows: ACROSS: 1. ETERNALLIFE, 8. JESUS, 10. ARIANISM, 11. CULT, 12. EAR, 13. CHRISTIANSCIENTIST, 15. MORMON, 16. EDDY, 17. RUSSELL; DOWN: 2. FORGIVENESS, 3. BIBLICAL, 4. HERESY, 5. NICENECREED, 6. PELAGIANISM, 7. JEHOVAHWITNESS, 9. SMITH, 14. COUNCIL.

Ask, **What did Paul warn in Acts 20:29?** Paul said, **I know that after I leave, savage wolves will come in among you and will not spare the flock.** Then ask, **Who are the wolves to whom Paul refers? Who are the flock?** The wolves are those people who will spread false teachings about the person and work of Jesus. The flock consists of believers in Jesus.

What does Jesus teach in Matt. 7:15–16? The outward appearance of false teachers will hide their ravenous desire to destroy faith.

INTRODUCTION TO THE "NEW" CULTS

Ask a student volunteer to read the first two paragraphs of this section.

Discuss the following questions: **Why is it important to study how cults emerged from the Jesus-people movement? In what ways do you think these cults were more attractive than the traditional Christian church? Why might cults be attractive to young people? In what ways was the Jesus-people movement good? In what ways was the movement dangerous?**

The Jesus-people movement was good in that it stressed a personal relationship with Jesus Christ and encouraged believers to witness their faith. It was dangerous since many cults were formed by strong leaders who often replaced God's authority with their own.

Introduce the cults that will be studied in this session by reading the remainder of this section. Then discuss the following questions: **What do cults offer that make them appealing to Christians?** Cults offer extreme lifestyles, either free and easy or rigid and controlled. **What dangers do cult recruiters pose for the Christian?** Cult recruiters often use empty promises or lies to attract new recruits.

THE FAMILY OF LOVE

Remind students that during every period of history groups of people become disillusioned with society and try to escape. Ask, **How might people try to escape the problems of life?** Some abuse drugs and alcohol. Others form isolated communities away from the problems of cities and urban areas.

Have students read this section in the Student Book. In suggesting that cult members change their names, Berg sought to give them new identities and bond them together into a new community, set apart from the rest of the world.

Most cults ignore God's Word and attack the person and work of Jesus. Ask, **What happens to Christians when they are urged to believe in or do things which God's Word forbids? How can cult leaders become the supreme authority in a group? What can you do to guard against being caught and trapped by cult leaders who have established themselves as supreme authority over God and His Word?**

Read **1 John 4:1.** We test "spirits" by asking questions about what they say concerning Jesus Christ. For example, suggest that students use the following questions to determine the teachings of a cult. What does a group believe about Christ's substitutionary death and triumphant resurrection? Do the leaders accept these as historical events or do they interpret them only symbolically?

Ask, **What type of people are attracted to an authoritarian cult leader?** The umbrella of authority offered by most cult leaders is very attractive to people who are dependent and don't want to make decisions for themselves. People who are insecure and afraid are susceptible to recruitment by cults.

Ask, **How would you witness to members of a group like the Children of God who encourage you to follow Moses David's commands without question? What if the group leader told your wife or mother to go "flirty fishing?" Could you locate Scripture passages which forbid such activity?**

What do you do when someone teaches something that conflicts with God's Word? Direct students to read **Acts 5:29.** Then discuss the following questions: **How do you know whether you are being asked to follow God or a person? What do you say to someone who attempts to trick you?** Remind students that whenever they are confronted by a cult member they have an opportunity to witness their faith in Jesus as their Savior from sin, death, and the power of the devil.

THE MOONIES

Before reading this section ask students the following questions: **Who are the Moonies? Who is the ultimate authority for the Moonies?** Tell students that after reading this section in the Student Book they will be able to answer these and other questions about the Moonies. Like the Mormons, the Moonies suggest that Moon's teachings are more authoritative than Holy Scripture. Moonies respect and follow the information given Moon during his alleged vision of Christ above and before the Bible. Moon claims to be a better, more perfect revelation than Jesus.

While the Unification Church still exists in Korea, it is most successful in the United States. Ask students, **Why is the Unification Church so successful in the United States?** We have great religious freedom. Cults have free access into people's homes through mail, radio, and television. Many Americans are bored with life and seek diversion. The strong control methods imposed by cult leaders resemble the mind control techniques used by the Chinese Communists who brainwashed American soldiers during World War II. The Communists deprogrammed soldiers' brains through constant repetition and by isolating their victims from those who would dissuade them.

What would you do if you suspect a cult member is trying to sell something to you? If you knew a cult tended to lie about their identity, how could you discover the truth? What could you say and do? How might you witness your faith in Jesus?

What might you say to someone who said that Jesus failed in the task God had assigned Him to complete while on the earth? Rev. Moon claims he is finishing the task Jesus failed to complete. Moonies speak of physical redemption. The Bible teaches about spiritual redemption for eternity purchased by Christ's blood. Read **1 Peter 1:18, Heb. 7:26–27,** and **1 John 2:1–2.** Compare these passages from God's Word with Moon's teachings.

Discuss "deprogramming," a technique which some parents have used to get their children out of cults. Although generally unsubstantiated, some deprogramming is accomplished through violence. There is also a danger that once deprogrammed an individual may be wary of putting trust in any religious leader or religious organization. Discuss how the saying, "Once bitten, twice shy," applies in this situation. Ask, **What can be done to win these people's trust so that they will listen to you as you share the Good News of Jesus Christ?**

THE WAY INTERNATIONAL

Ask students to volunteer to read portions of this section in the Student Book. Ask, **Why is an invitation to attend a Bible study a sneaky way of involving people in a cult?** Unlike other cults which "kidnap" young people, this group involves even high-school-aged people while they are still living at home.

Ask, **What is wrong with attending a class in which you can't ask questions or take notes?** This is a very manipulative and unfair practice.

Study **1 Tim. 2:5** with your students. **How does Wierwille use this passage to argue against the doctrine of the Trinity?** He takes it out of the context of all of Scripture.

Wierwille encourages "speaking in tongues," but not as a spiritual gift **(1 Cor. 12:10, 28; 14:6–19).** Wierwille teaches people to speak in an ecstatic language rather than exercising a real spiritual gift from God. Contrary to Scripture, he also requires speaking in tongues to maintain membership in his church.

Like most cults, The Way International denies the deity of Christ. Christians can point to many Scripture passages in which Jesus is ascribed the attributes of God **(Matt. 9:2–6; Mark 2:5; Acts 4:12; Phil. 2:9–11; John 1:1–2; Col. 1:16).** Witnessing to a member of The Way International may be difficult, but not impossible. They twist Scripture to fit their own teaching, so you must be sure to study the entire context in which a particular verse is located. Help your students locate verses which clearly describe the deity and blood sacrifice of Jesus Christ on the cross. Suggest that students memorize the passages listed previously.

SCIENTOLOGY

Ask, **Has anyone seen a television commercial for a book called *Dianetics*?** This is L. Ron Hubbard's "bible." In it Hubbard denies nearly every Biblical doctrine including salvation by grace through faith in Christ Jesus.

Ask for a volunteer to read this section or direct the students to read silently this section of the Student Book.

Hubbard cannot prove he has the credentials which he claims for himself in his book. With the attaching of a simple voltmeter to measure the surface resistance of the skin, Scientologist "auditors" claim to counsel people to become "clear." Their counselors ask and make suggestions until the meter registers "clear." People are in love with this "quick-fix." Many people pay great sums of money to receive this healing. Ask, **Do you think it is really a healing? Is it from God?**

Hubbard renamed his organization "The Church of Scientology" in order to gain tax-exempt status.

This probably benefited Hubbard personally and since his death has helped many members of his church. Although Scientologists claim to accept the Bible as the Word of God, they elevate Hubbard's writings far above the Bible.

HARE KRISHNA

Read and discuss this section of the Student Book.

Unlike the other cults discussed in this session, Hare Krishna splintered from the Hindu religion. While Hindus have worshiped Krishna for centuries, it was only when the Swami emigrated to the United States that his teachings took on a Christian and western flavor in order to attract Christians.

Hare Krishnas preach inner peace attainable through "enlightenment." Krishnas are also devoted to fund raising. They have recently been encountered in "disguise" in many United States national parks. They are "disguised" because they have exchanged their robes for more traditional American dress.

When initiated into the group, Krishnas are given a "mantra" and told to repeat it softly and silently in a meditative attempt to empty their minds. Read **Matt. 12:43–45**. Ask, **How could emptying your mind be dangerous?** If you could truly empty your mind, there is a danger that Satan or one of his evil spirits could enter. Doubts and fears about your faith in Christ could replace a once strong faith. A potential Krishna recruit with an empty mind could easily be convinced to follow a strong cult leader.

Read **Phil. 4:8**. There are better things than a "mantra" to think about. Ask the class to brainstorm several suggestions of things which they could think about which might serve to strengthen their faith.

The peace offered by Jesus is forgiveness of sins **(Matt 11:28–29)** and the assurance of eternal life **(John 11:25–26)**. No other religion offers this kind of hope.

THE BAITED AND BARBED HOOK!

Ask, **How are cults like bait and a fish hook?** While cults may appear very attractive, they are extremely deadly. Those who are lured by bait usually are caught because the bait hides the potential dangers.

The bait on a fish hook covers the barb until it is too late. The barb on a fish hook prevents the fish from escaping. Cults have a similar barb which discourages new recruits from leaving. Once recruited with flashy promises, cult members commit themselves to a cause and believe in it. It is unlikely that they will leave on their own. Unaware of the way they are manipulated and controlled, cult members will sacrifice everything to a leader who is cheating, controlling, and using them.

Read **Rom. 12:1–2**. Ask, **To whom have the people of God committed themselves?**

Review ways in which people might look for a quick fix as a solution to their problems. Solutions might include drugs and alcohol. Quick-fix solutions are suggested in subtle ways in advertising. Ask students to generate a list of ads which offer a quick fix. For example, "Got a headache? Take two of our pills."

With recent technological advances we are accustomed to having everything quickly and easily. Cult leaders like Jim Jones (People's Temple) seek to solve complex problems such as racism and sexism in simple ways. These solutions backfire. But few problems which have existed for a long time will disappear easily, quickly, or completely through the efforts of any human leader. The only cure for society's problems is found in God's Word.

TO REVIEW AND REMEMBER

Continue to lead students in a review of the three articles of the Apostles' Creed and their explanation.

FAMILY TIME

Encourage students to read and discuss the activities suggested in the Student Book. Remind and encourage parents to work on these activities with their children.

ENRICHMENT ACTIVITIES

1. Ask students to react to the following scene.

Imagine you are the parent of a young person who was seduced into a cult. Your son or daughter was invited to a free dinner and informational meeting. The meeting was quickly followed by a very attractive-sounding weekend retreat, which was also followed by a week- or month-long field trip. The field trip turned out to be a cult indoctrination camp in which certain authority and controls were placed over new recruits, so that when the camp was over, they didn't want to return home. They were taught to offer total allegiance to the cult leader. Since family and former friends would only try to remove them from this wonderful setting, they were warned against further contact with them. They were, in fact, encouraged to write or phone their former family and friends and renounce all connection with them.

As the parent who receives such a letter or call, how would you react? Would you be angry? scared? What if you repeatedly tried to recontact your child, only to reach a dead end? How would you then react? Would you consider contacting a deprogrammer? For a sum of money these people would kidnap your child from the cult and spend a great deal of time and effort to return him/her to his/her former state.

2. Advertising often offers a quick-fix solution to such problems as bad breath, body odor, illness, blemishes, etc. Cut out advertisements from magazines and newspapers which offer a quick fix. Glue these ads onto a piece of construction paper to make a montage. After the page is filled with advertisements, write with a marking pen the words "Jesus Is the Only Way."

3. Following the model used in television advertising, direct students to write a script for a radio or television commercial for Jesus. Direct students to answer the question, "Who is Jesus Christ?" in their script. Tape record or videotape the commercials.

4. Ask students to design a maze in which each of the dead ends is one of the cults studied in this session or a previous session. Direct students to symbolize the exit of the maze with a cross. Allow students to share their mazes with other students.

CLOSING WORSHIP

Use the section in the Student Book entitled "Jesus Never Changes" as a closing devotion. God always provides forgiveness to the penitent sinner through faith in Jesus. Offer a prayer of thanks and praise for God's mercy in Christ Jesus.

Satanic Cults

DISCOVERY POINT

When Jesus conquered sin, death, and the power of the devil, God demonstrated His supreme authority and power over Satan, the counterfeiter, who copies God and tries to lead God's people away from the truth.

OBJECTIVES

That by the power of the Spirit working through God's Word the students will

1. confess the victory Christ earned for them from sin, death, and the power of the devil by His death and resurrection;
2. describe the evil and spiritual nature of Satan's attacks on them and all people;
3. describe the activity of satanic groups;
4. use the means of grace which God graciously provides so that they can withstand Satan's trickery;
5. identify Satan's strategies in attempting to destroy people's faith in Christ Jesus.

MATERIALS

- [ ] Bibles
- [ ] Student Book
- [ ] *Lutheran Worship* or *The Lutheran Hymnal*
- [ ] Pens or pencils

Optional
- [ ] poster board
- [ ] markers
- [ ] notebook paper
- [ ] newspaper or magazine stories
- [ ] newsprint
- [ ] concordance
- [ ] *How to Respond to Satanism,* available from CPH
- [ ] *How to Respond to the New Age Movement,* available from CPH

OPENING WORSHIP

Read **1 John 4:4** and tell students that Satan is real and in the world. He may even disguise himself as someone good, perhaps even "an angel of light" **(2 Cor. 11:13–14)**.

The Holy Spirit who dwells in all believers is also very real. The warfare is spiritual, and therefore the opponent is invisible **(Eph. 6:12)**. Both God and Satan possess great power, but God's power is superior to that of Satan. The warfare between these forces is spiritual, and therefore each opponent is invisible **(Eph. 6:12)**.

God didn't remain invisible. He came in the flesh. He became a human like us, lived among us, and died for us so that we, too, can have life. With knowledge of the promise of His presence we can "resist the devil, and he will flee from you" **(James 4:7)**.

Tell students that when they become aware of the invisible spiritual warfare which rages about them, they can and must call upon God for His help, for He has promised them His continual love, presence, and protection.

Close the worship portion of the lesson with a prayer, asking God for guidance, protection, and direction. The children of Israel were protected by the blood of the lamb at the first Passover **(Heb. 9:13–14)**. Claim God's protection by the power of the blood of Jesus.

INTRODUCING THE LESSON

1. Ask students to draw a picture of Satan on newsprint. Have students discuss their drawings. Explain to students that it is difficult to draw pictures of Satan, because he is invisible. We have a number of pictures of Satan from Scripture—a serpent **(Gen. 3:1)**, a tempter **(Matt. 4:1)**, a roaring lion **(1 Peter 5:8)**, and a dragon **(Rev. 12:3, 20:2)**. These are simply pictures to describe a dangerous enemy. Brainstorm suggestions to help you recognize Satan and his tricks in order to defend yourself against him.

2. As students arrive divide the class into groups. Have each group locate as many Bible passages as they can that mention the devil or evidence of his presence. You may wish to provide students with a concordance in order to complete this activity. If you have not already done so, teach students how to use a concordance. After a few minutes have students share their lists. Make a master list of passages on the chalkboard or overhead projector. Suggest that students copy and keep a complete list for further reference.

3. Ask for examples of newspaper, magazine, television, or radio news stories which mention Satanism, the occult, or some other kind of ritual worship. Discuss the stories and encourage students to bring copies of such stories to class. Talk about how some of the stories may be sensationalized, especially those included in supermarket tabloids. Ask, **Are there ways to determine if certain news stories are legitimate or fake?** Discuss with students the importance of knowing the reliability of the source and checking it out with other sources.

Warn students against undue fear or anxiety over stories of satanic activity. Some students become uneasy and have nightmares after studying this topic. Point out that although Satan is strong, Christ is stronger. On the cross Jesus said, **"It is finished"** **(John 19:30).** His victory for us is complete. The payment for sin and eternal life is assured for all who believe and trust in Him.

MEANING FOR LIFE

Have students read **1 Cor. 12:1–13.** Ask, **How has God's Spirit been working in your life since you were born?** God has gifted each of us with His Spirit through the means of grace.

Ask, **What is life?** Discuss various answers, but point out that "real" life is only that which is connected to God, the Giver of life. Jesus said, **"The thief comes only to steal and kill and destroy; I have come that you may have life, and have it to the full" (John 10:10).**

Some people believe that God began the world and wound it up like a large clock, but that He has simply left it to run down and no longer cares about it. Ask, **How do you know that God really cares about you and the world today?** Discuss God's answer to their prayers and the encouragement they receive when they read the Bible.

Ask students to volunteer to read portions of **Luke 24:13–35.** Then ask, **Have any of you ever had an experience like that of the disciples on the road to Emmaus?** After the disciples listened to Jesus, they asked one another, **"Were not our hearts burning within us while He talked with us on the road and opened the Scriptures to us?" (Luke 24:32).** Only by the power of the Holy Spirit working through God's Word can we truly know Jesus **(1 Cor. 12:3).**

Study **Psalm 139** together and answer questions from the Student Book. The Savior who knew us intimately before we were born and desires to always remain close to us, also has a will and specific plan for each of our lives.

A WAY THAT SEEMS RIGHT

Ask, **What is wrong with "thinking" in your heart that you know the right way?** By nature our minds are spiritually darkened **(2 Cor. 4:4).** Left to our own devices, we are doomed for death and eternal separation from God **(Rom. 5:10).** Read **Prov. 14:12** and discuss the many times we "think" we know the right way. We are certain that we are correct. In the end it turns out that we are "dead" wrong, because we are reasoning with minds infected with sin. We can only know the truth through Christ. In fact, Christ is the Truth.

Focus not on the lack of decisive Biblical information about Satan's origin, but rather the clarity of Christ's victory over Satan and all evil. God calls Satan an angel of light **(2 Cor. 11:14),** the father of lies **(John 8:44),** and Beelzebub, the prince of demons **(Matt. 12:27).**

Rev. 12:7–9 describes a battle between Satan and God's angels. Satan's eternal banishment is described in **Rev. 20:7–10.**

SATAN TRICKS ADAM AND EVE

Satan tempts us to doubt God's Word just as he led Adam and Eve to doubt God's words and promises. Ask, **How can Satan tempt us to doubt God's Word?** Satan tempts us to doubt the following: specific parts of the Bible (creation, the flood, Christ's death and resurrection), God's love and care for us, the reality of God's existence, presence, and power. Ultimately, this doubt is faith-threatening.

2. Similarly, Satan contradicts the Bible. Satan is a great mimic or counterfeiter. He enjoys doing everything just the opposite from God, but making it look like God has done it. Ask, **What good things from God has Satan soiled?** Satan has soiled food, drink, sexuality, truth, friendships, etc. Point out that when aware of Satan's tricks, we can withstand his attacks even though he will continue to strike.

Satan's promise of immortality is not very attractive when students consider that the life Satan offers is without God.

3. One of Satan's greatest tricks is to suggest that we will be just like God. This is a philosophy promoted by the New Age movement. A good resource concerning the New Age movement is *How to Respond*

to the New Age Movement by Philip Lochhaas (St. Louis: CPH, 1988). The New Age movement is humanistic idealism. It suggests that all human problems can be solved if people realize and accept that they are gods.

Contrast Satan's lie with your own experience **(Ezek. 18:4, 20)**. Ask, **Do you know anyone who will not die? What does Jesus' resurrection from the dead say about our life and death?**

SATAN ATTACKS JESUS

1. At times we may think that since we are Christians Satan can't or won't attack us. Actually, he more actively attacks Christians since he already controls all other people. If Satan was bold enough to attack Jesus, what makes us think that he won't attack us?

In his first temptation Satan tempted Jesus to obey him and feed (serve) Himself. Ask, **Does the temptation to look out for number one exist in your lives?** Selfishness is a popular temptation of Satan. While it is not satanic to serve ourselves, it becomes satanic when it consumes our entire existence.

2. Similarly, Satan tempts us to abandon God's plan to use wisely the gifts He gives us. Satan would have us do anything rather than serve and obey God. He must especially dislike it when we share God's Good News of salvation with other people.

3. Satan offered Jesus the world in exchange for His worship of him. As Satan wanted to be worshiped then, he wants us to worship him now.

God promised that Jesus would suffer and die to earn forgiveness of sins and eternal life for all people. Satan often tempts us by suggesting that we can and should win the world without suffering. Read and discuss **Is. 53:3** and **Acts 14:22**. Often we may strive to set goals for our lives in which we attempt to avoid all suffering and pain.

4. Satan's main temptation is to try to convince us that God could never love us because of our sin. Ask, **Have you ever doubted that you are a child of God? How often and when do these temptations come?** These temptations usually come when we feel the guilt of our sin. Satan wants us to believe that God couldn't love someone as vile as we.

Remind students that Jesus used God's Word when tempted by the devil. God's Word will give us the power to resist the temptation of the devil just as it strengthened Jesus. Talk about ways students can remain in God's Word through devotions, Bible study, and worship. Ask, **Why is God's Word called the "sword of the Spirit" (Eph. 6:17)?** When tempted to sin, God's Spirit uses God's Word to help us ward off Satan's attacks.

Discuss how in praying the 7th petition of the Lord's Prayer, "deliver us from evil," we are asking God to keep us from the Evil One, Satan.

Although a defeated enemy, Satan still prowls, seeking to destroy us through one or all of the tactics he used on Jesus. We must be on the lookout and resist him by the power of the Holy Spirit working through the Word.

SAY YOU LOVE SATAN

After reading the quote from *Newsweek*, ask students to comment. Reports like this are indeed frightening.

SATAN TRIES TO ECLIPSE GOD

Ask, **How does Satan try to disguise himself in your life?** He makes anger and revenge seem good and acceptable. He turns good into evil, perverting food, sexuality, ordinary speech, etc. Ask students to name as many of Satan's disguises as possible.

Scripture warns us that some will abandon their faith and follow deceiving spirits **(1 Tim. 4:1)**, there will be terrible times in the last days **(2 Tim. 3:1)**, and many false prophets will appear and deceive many people **(Matt. 24:10–12)**.

RELIGIOUS SATANISTS

A good history of Satanism and an introduction to contemporary satanic practices are provided in *How to Respond to Satanism* by Bruce Frederickson (St. Louis: CPH, 1988).

Ask, **Why do you think Aleister Crowley behaved in the way he did?** He was a sinner, and therefore naturally inclined away from God and His will. Crowley sought to satisfy his sinful nature through excessive sex, alcohol, and other forms of "pleasure." Although some modern, non-Christian scholars dispute his involvement in Satanism, the things he did and the organizations he started indicate that his beliefs were directly opposed to God.

THE FIRST CHURCH OF SATAN

Provide the following background information concerning the life of Anton Szandor LaVey.

LaVey was born in 1930. His middle European grandparents told stories of witches and vampires from their native Transylvania. By age five LaVey had read the rather strange stories of *Frankenstein* and *Dracula*.

During World War II, he became interested in modern warfare concluding that contrary to the Bible, the earth could be inherited by the mighty, rather than the meek.

LaVey did most of his serious studying after school hours on topics which his friends found strange. He was deeply interested in studying metaphysics, the occult, and music. At age 15 he played oboe in the San Francisco Ballet Symphony Orchestra. Bored with his regular studies, he dropped out of school before graduation and joined the Clyde Beatty Circus.

At age 18, he left the circus and joined a carnival. As assistant to a magician, he learned hypnosis and continued studying the occult. He saw life as something in which youth, vigor, and strength were worshiped. The old and weak were weeded out like last year's fashions. Recalling his carnival days, he said:

I would see men lusting after half-naked girls dancing at the carnival, and on Sunday morning when I was playing organ for tent-show evangelists at the other end of the carnival lot, I would see these same men sitting in the pews with their wives and children, asking God to forgive them and purge them of carnal desires. And the next Saturday night they'd be back at the carnival or some other place of indulgence. I knew then that the Christian church thrives on hypocrisy, and that man's carnal nature will win out no matter how much it is purged or scourged by any white-light religion. (Introduction to *The Satanic Bible*, by Burton H. Wolfe, [Avon, NY], 1969.)

LaVey did not intend to found a "new" religion. Satanism is very old. But LaVey's great contribution to Satanism was to formalize it into specific thoughts and rituals.

After his marriage at the age of 20, he settled down to train for a career. He studied criminology at the City College of San Francisco and became a photographer for the San Francisco Police Department. Again, he witnessed life at its worst. "I saw the bloodiest, grimiest side of human nature," LaVey recounted. "It was disgusting and depressing. I asked myself: 'Where is God?' I came to detest the sanctimonious attitude of people toward violence, always saying 'it was God's will.'" (Introduction to *The Satanic Bible*.)

LaVey quit his job with the police department and played the organ in nightclubs and theaters. He continued his study of the black arts. He led a weekly class on a college campus where he taught occult arts, hauntings, E.S.P., vampires, divination, and satanic worship. His regular students were probably attracted as much to LaVey as to the subject. Soon a "Magic Circle" evolved from this group.

LaVey accumulated a vast library of books about medieval occult practices. He was amused by people who blasphemed and made fun of the Christian church in secret ceremonies held by his group. LaVey considered Satan a kind of humanly and physically recognizable force that was responsible for the way people acted.

On April 30, 1966, during "Walpurgisnacht," one of the most important festivals in witchcraft, LaVey shaved his head and announced the formation of the Church of Satan. LaVey wore a clerical collar and black suit in order to be properly identified as a minister.

All other churches worshiped a spirit and denied the flesh and intellect. According to LaVey, the satanic church would recapture the minds of people and allow them to use their fleshly desires as a cause for celebration, instead of struggle.

Rather than mock Christianity with the "Black Mass," he invented celebrations consecrating special events. People asked for satanic weddings and funerals. These weddings allowed participants to celebrate the joy of fleshly pleasure. During LaVey's most popular ritual, a destruction ritual, participants curse and celebrate triumph over their enemies.

Producers of the movie, *Rosemary's Baby*, which was about Satan, engaged LaVey's services as technical consultant. LaVey calls this story about a young girl whose baby was fathered by Satan, one of the best advertisements for Satanism since the inquisition.

After reading the Nine Satanic Statements, compare them with the Ten Commandments. Compare LaVey's ideas with God's expectations.

Ask, **Are LaVey's teachings dangerous? Why or why not?**

SATANIC CULTS/SELF-STYLED SATANISTS

Because of their nature, information about these groups is rather sketchy, has questionable reliability, and is difficult to piece together.

There are strong suggestions that many of these groups are closely related. In his book *The Ultimate Evil*, Maury Terry, a New York news reporter, suggests a direct connection between David Berkowitz, the "Son of Sam" murders in Manhattan, and the Charles Manson murders in California. He describes the similarities between the beliefs, methods, and goals of these two groups. There are strong suggestions that these two groups splintered from the once visible and now underground group called "The Process Church of the Final Judgment." This group believed that judgment day would be hastened by the violence and murder they initiated.

Discuss fantasy roleplaying games such as *Dungeons and Dragons* with students. Talk about some parts of the game, such as the casting of spells, death curses, and other practices which are clearly forbidden by God in Scripture. As time permits share the following information:

1. Enchantments—influence by charms and magic arts, **Lev. 19:26; Deut. 18:10–12; 2 Kings 17:17; 2 Chron. 33:6; Jer. 27:9; Daniel 1:20.**

2. Witchcraft/Magic/Sorcery/Wizardry—dealing with spirits of the dead, using power gained from the assistance or control of evil spirits, **Ex. 22:18; Deut.**

18:10–12; 1 Sam. 15:23; 2 Kings 17:17; 2 Chron. 33:6; Is. 47:9; Jer. 27:8–9; Gal. 5:19–21; Rev. 21:8.

3. Divination/Soothsaying/Prognostication—fortunetelling, prophesying events by a spirit other than the Holy Spirit, **Deut. 18:10–12; Joshua 13:22; 2 Kings 17:17; Is. 47:12–15; Jer. 27:8–9, 29:8–9; Micah 5:12–15; Acts 16:16–24.**

4. Necromancy—communicating with the dead, conjuring spirits of the dead to gain information about unknown things and the future, or an attempt to influence the course of history, **Deut. 18:11; 1 Chron. 10:13–14.**

5. Charm—putting a spell on someone or effecting something by magic, **Deut. 19:11; Is. 19:36.**

6. Stargazing/Astrology—the "supposed" influence of stars on human affairs and earthly events, **Lev. 19:26; Deut. 19:10–14; 2 Kings 21:6; 2 Chron. 33:6; Is. 47:12–15; Jer. 10:2; Daniel 1:18–20, 4:1–37, 5:7–15.**

WHAT TO DO ABOUT SATANISM

Discuss the exorcism which occurs at the beginning of many traditional Lutheran baptismal services. Ask, **How can your baptism be compared to the beginning of your spiritual warfare against Satan?**

Discuss ways to resist Satan. Remind students of the importance of studying Scripture to know exactly how Satan works and to receive the strength the Holy Spirit offers to resist him.

Talk about how "give him an inch and he will take a mile" is an appropriate description of Satan.

TO REVIEW AND REMEMBER

Read the Scripture passages. Ask students, **How can you put God's armor on?** Recall with students that when Jesus was arrested Peter followed closely and went into the midst of his enemies **(Matt. 26:57–75)**. He was tempted and denied Jesus. Perhaps when we recognize our weaknesses, we should avoid people and places in which Satan can tempt us.

FAMILY TIME

Assign one or more of the activities. Suggest that the activities be used as family devotional material.

ENRICHMENT ACTIVITIES

1. Draw Satan-buster posters. Suggest that students include symbols for the means of grace, God's Word and His Sacraments, on the posters.

2. Ask students to prepare a witness of their faith to a person who claims to be a satanist. Brainstorm possible objections or questions a Satanist may use when confronted with a Christian witness.

3. Have students write a report comparing the methods Satan used in tempting Jesus with the methods he uses in tempting us. Urge students to give specific examples.

4. Ask students to write a news story for a newspaper or a radio broadcast urging people to resist Satan's temptations. Students may wish to call the story "Satan Prowls—Emergency News Bulletin." After news stories are complete, ask students to present them to the class.

CLOSING WORSHIP

Affirm the power of God's Word by rereading **Matt. 4:11.**

Sing or say the words of the simple, but appropriate song, "Jesus Loves Me."

Conclude with a prayer asking God to help and protect you and your students against Satan.

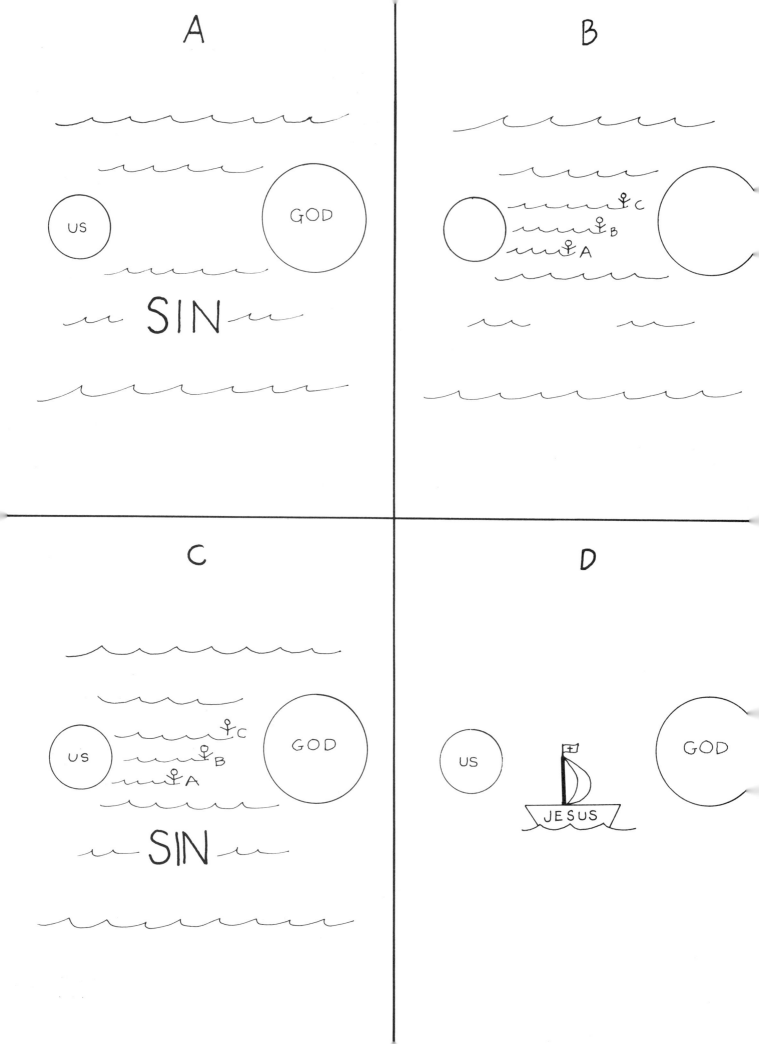

JUNIOR HIGH MINI-COURSES

Cults and Other Beliefs
Makes students aware of differences between Christianity, various cults, and pseudo-Christian religions.

Managing My Free Time
Prepares students to effectively deal with peer pressure, the media, music, and drugs.

Managing My Life
Helps students make wise choices with God's gifts of family, time and talents, sexuality, and more.

Those Others and Me
Helps students see the difference they can make in the plight of the poor, the hungry, the lonely, the homeless, and more.

What About AIDS?
Encourages students to respond in God's love to AIDS victims and presents them with the facts on this deadly disease.

God's Faithful Witnesses
Encourages students to make their lives count for Christ by examining the lives of Athanasius, Augustine, Luther, and Walther.

Worship: Celebrating God's Grace
Helps students appreciate their Lutheran heritage by comparing Lutheran worship to the worship of other denominations.

© 1990 Concordia   H52767

If you like this Mini-Course, we have six more in store...

...Six more mini-courses that present key Bible concepts and contemporary issues in just four sessions each—an ideal way to maximize your 6th through 8th grade curriculum.

Whether you teach day/weekday school, Sunday School or confirmation class, you'll find these mini-courses are great ways to enhance and supplement your regular curriculum.

Examine them first hand by calling for a sample pak which includes a Student Guide of each mini-course *(except What About AIDS?)*

ORDER YOUR SAMPLE PAK TODAY!
22-2397DHAQ ———————— $7.95
(plus postage & handling)

CALL 1-800-325-3040

Also available at your Christian bookstore.

Make Bible Memory Work Simple, Memorable, and Sharable

Teach Bible concepts in an unforgettable way with the *Key Chapters of the Bible Learning Plan*, by Paul Schroeder.

This Learning Plan provides materials based on simple drawings that help participants remember the importance of key Bible passages. It's ideal for youth and adult confirmation, adult Bible classes, Sunday School, day and weekday school. Participants use flash cards and coordinated materials—all with clever artwork and brief copy—to learn concepts of Scripture and memorize key Bible passages.

What makes *Key Chapters* work so well? The concepts are...

1 *Simple.* Unique illustrations with one key idea present important Bible concepts clearly.

2 *Memorable.* The imaginative illustrations are a humorous and unforgettable way to picture key concepts. They make an impression that breaks through the clutter of messages each person receives daily.

3 *Sharable.* Key Chapters enables participants to remember Biblical concepts so they're better prepared to share their faith when witnessing opportunities arise.

Key Chapters of the Bible—An Unforgettable Learning Plan contains:
- 20 flash cards
- One poster showing every illustration
- Two books the leader uses to fully explain the concept
- One User's Guide.

22-2393DHAS *Key Chapters Learning Plan* _____ **$26.95**

CONCORDIA® PUBLISHING HOUSE
3558 SOUTH JEFFERSON AVENUE
SAINT LOUIS, MISSOURI 63118-3968

For more information or to order, visit your Christian bookstore or call **1-800-325-3040** today!

22-2346
0-570-09753-3